10 Powerful Networking Tips Using Business
Cards Global Extended Edition

Copyright Carl E. Reid 2014

Published by SAVVY INTRPRENEUR
Publishing at Smashwords

Library of Congress

ISBN-13: 978-1500550967
ISBN-10: 1500550965

* Please Write a Review of This Book at*

Thank you SO MUCH for taking time out of
your busy schedule to write a review of this
book. Your review is an important
contribution to helping SAVVY
INTRAPRENUER improve the global world
around us, one professional at a time. Good or

bad, your feedback helps improve the quality
of information shared.

Other Books by Carl E. Reid, CSI

*10 Powerful Networking Secrets Of
Influential People*

101 Ways To Be Fearless At Work

Foreword Author of
Win The Race For 21ˢᵗ Century Jobs by Rod
Colón

This book is dedicated to . . .

All the volunteers, leaders and members of Empowering Today's Professionals. Also to any person who is new to networking or a lifetime student trying to master the art and etiquette of networking.

Contents

Foreword by Rod Colón...................................6

What is a Savvy Intrapreneur? 8

Introduction 10

How Did This Business Card Thing Get
Started?...12

What's the Big Deal Today with Business
Cards?...14

1. Never Leave Home Without Them 15

2. Use Proper Business Card Etiquette.........17

    Business Card Design Preparation............18

    Translations...19

    Hiearchy 19

    Acknowledgements 19

    When Giving Out Your Business Card . . .
   19

    Receiving a Business Card 20

3. Be Generous 20

4. Ask for Referrals 22

5. Maximize Every Per Chance Meeting 23

6. Place Yourself at the Right Place at the
Right Time 24

7. Use Email as Your Electronic Business
Card 26

8. Use In Your Face Follow Up 27

9. Leverage Staff Promotions to Promote ME,
Inc 29

10. Brand Yourself With a Slogan 30

Networking on Social Media......................31

Life and Networking Go Together 32

Stop Networking. Start Living. 34

VIDEO BONUS - How to Gain Strength
from Your Network in Challenging Times ..36

About Author: Carl E. Reid.......................37

CONNECT with Carl 38

Foreword by Rod Colón

Key to managing your career as a business is understanding the power of a business card. The branding, sharing and leveraging of business cards is often an overlooked process. Carl E. Reid has done a great service by explaining how to brand yourself on a business card and explaining the art of leveraging business cards as we manage our career as a business. His tested and proven techniques in "10 Powerful Networking Tips Using Business Cards" is a must read and reference manual for all students and professionals. Carl's diverse career as a business owner, career professional and business coach positions him perfectly in delivering this wonderful handbook.

Every student and professional determined to own their career must have copy of this great tool – "*10 Powerful Networking Tips Using Business Cards Global Extended Edition*."

Rod Colón

Master Networker, Professional Development, Executive Coach, Speaker, Author and Founder of Empowering Today's

Professionals
Rod Colón Consulting, LLC
Tel: 732-367-5580
www.RodColon.com
Call in to Rod's weekly radio show *Own Your Career*
www.blogtalkradio.com/OwnYourCareer

What is a Savvy Intrapreneur?

The first question people ask me regarding my workshops or free newsletter is "what is a Savvy Intrapreneur?" First, let's answer the question "What is an Intrapreneur?"

Gifford Pinchot coined the word "Intrapreneur" in the 70s. Gifford was and still is ahead of his time in vision. An Intrapreneur thinks like an entrepreneur seeking out opportunities, which benefit the corporation. It was a new way of thinking, in making companies more productive and profitable. IBM was one of the 1st companies to execute the Intrapreneur approach, when it spun off a separate company as its personal computer division, in the early 80s. The entire leadership of the new company was made up entirely of Intrapreneurs. Risk taking, visionary employees who thought like entrepreneurs.

A Savvy Intrapreneur takes a good idea and makes it better.

A Savvy Intrapreneur steps out of the comfort zone of corporate security, to insure s/he creates additional income which at least matches their take home pay. An Intrapreneur works overtime helping to run someone else's business, for the company's future. A Savvy Intrapreneur runs themselves like a profitable business putting in 1 hour a day of overtime for their own financial future.

Developing a career while maintaining position at work requires staying focused as a Savvy Intrapreneur. This takes courage.

Are you ready?

Then step out. Dare to make yourself "fireproof" at work.

Introduction

I first published the information shared in this book in 2004, as a short article. According to Google, the article went viral onto thousands of web sites, blogs and social media networks.

Many thanks to the Los Angeles Chinese Learning Center, Rod Colon Consulting, Net-Temps, Ezine Articles, iPower Global Solutions, Asian Business Cards and Scott Ginsberg for being prominent champions to publish the original article.

The world has become smaller. Developing personal and business networking relationships requires acting local, but thinking global. The changing world landscape of diverse cultures now surrounds us down to your next door neighbors. Career and business survival dictates learning savvy approaches and etiquette for using business cards in various situations.

This book focuses on proven ways to make lasting impressions and capture attention using business cards. It follows that old cliché that "you don't get a 2nd chance to make a 1st impression". This may mean a little extra thought, consideration and expense in designing your business card. Similar to targeted resumes getting more calls for job interviews, you want the person receiving your business card to say to themselves "s/he [meaning you] understands me or is like me".

Having your business initiate a relationship is a powerful transaction that takes a few seconds, but creates an unforgettable branding experience that could last a lifetime. The goal of planned and unplanned meetings is to leverage the indelible power of a business card in creating a memorable, lasting impression, long after the meeting is over. This makes the follow up easier.

How Did This Business Card Thing Get Started?

In 17th century Europe it started as an aristocratic social tool when calling on a person at home. People would have very decorative trays placed in their entrance. Upon a visitor entering or leaving, a contact card would be left in that prominently displayed tray.

When the 18th and 19th centuries rolled around, these social introduction cards were presented by a lady or gentleman when it was her first time visit to a house. That fancy card tray was offered as soon as someone stepped through the door entrance. The visitor was expected to place their card in the tray as a show of etiquette. This card was then delivered to the person of the house. The card was carefully examined prior to receiving the visitor. Talk about making a first impression as a mandatory socially acceptable process. By the 19th century all middle class people, who wanted to establish themselves in social circles, would always present their social calling card.

And we think social media branding and marketing is a new concept of the 21st century.

What's the Big Deal Today with Business Cards?

Whether you are looking for a job or running a business, giving out business cards is crucial to marketing your skills or services. Even as a job seeker, develop the mindset of running the business of ME, Inc. Business cards speak volumes about who you are, what you offer and how serious you are marketing ME, Inc. as a business.

Oh! So, you have a resume and don't need business cards. Can you carry 10 resumes in your wallet? Do you or can you carry your resume everywhere you go? A church bell ringing lets people know they are open for business. Your business card is your bell. Here are some proven tips using business cards to increase your chances of landing a job or creating a business opportunity.

1. Never Leave Home Without Them

Before leaving home, your checklist should be expanded to include business cards, as part of "do I have my wallet/money, house keys, driver's license'" Any 'per chance' meeting is an opportunity to give out a business card. A morning run or a quick trip to the local store could be an opportunity to network. My wife and I always ask each other 'do you have business cards', before leaving the house. Make it a habit to carry business cards.

You just never know when the paths of 2 persons intersect how an opportunity can manifest itself. Carrying business cards as a habit also avoids embarrassment for those individuals who are in business for themselves, when someone asks for your business card. Having your business card at the ready adds credibility to really being an entrepreneur or serious business professional when meeting a stranger for the first time. Just pay for shipping and you can get free business cards at www.VistaPrint.com

I have beat myself up many times when meeting someone and not having a business card.

2. Use Proper Business Card Etiquette

In the United States, Canada and the UK business card etiquette is less formal. Whenever you give a business card, ask for a business card. When given a business card, don't just take it and place it in your pocket. Make the person feel important by looking at their card for a few seconds. You might see something that could be a topic of discussion. Write comments on the card such as date, location and common points of interest. These comments will prove valuable when following up with that person. This also demonstrates a sincere interest in the other person. Then place it in your wallet.

This lets people know they reside in a special place with you. "Skill with People" by Les Giblin is a book that expands on this approach. Make people feel important, in order to make yourself important to them. In other countries like India, Japan, China and Korea there is immense ceremonious formality or protocol associated with exchanging business cards. Make sure you do your homework to understand the cultural nuances when meeting with a particular group of people.

Business Card Design Preparation

The smart business professional treats the exchange of business cards with reverence and respect. If the tonality of the card layout aligns with local customs, this makes your hosts feel comfortable as a result of your considerate extra effort.

Make sure the card stock is of a high quality. This can suggest a high degree of success and prominence among many cultures. So spend time speaking with several business card suppliers. Get their professional recommendations on card stock selections. This will be time well spent.

Translations

Have your card professionally translated into the language of the country you intend to visit. The translation should be placed on the back of the card. This is expected in countries like Japan, Korea and China.

Hiearchy

Be aware of the pecking order in the food chain of an organization. In Japanese circles seniority is a well respected consideration, which you must acknowledge. Business cards should be left on the table, exposing the senior executive(s) cards closest to the top.

Acknowledgements

A snippet of degrees and professional qualifications printed on the card are expected in India and Latin American countries.

When Giving Out Your Business Card ...

Present your business card with language of your host country face up. Japanese and

Korean etiquette dictates using both hands to present your business card, with index finger and thumb on each corner. In Latin America and Japan business cards are exchanged during introductions with everyone at a meeting.

Be prepared that the business meeting may not happen for a couple of days in Latin American countries. So business cards are not given out during social interactions, which could be a quite a few over a couple of days

Receiving a Business Card . . .

Take time to look at the person's card. Try to find something to provide a sincere comment, compliment or commonality. Read and say the person's name out loud to confirm your pleasure in meeting this new person in your life.

3. Be Generous

Give business cards out to everyone, including family and friends. Don't let vanity stop you from giving out your last business card or giving 2 at a time to each person. I have met many people who have totally missed the purpose of a business card. I once asked a person for a second business card, so I could refer his services. His response was "I only have a few cards left and I need them", as he looked again at his name on the card. Hoarding your business cards only makes your wallet feel full, not your bank account.

4. Ask for Referrals

When giving a business card, people feel
more comfortable when you ask; 'I would
appreciate a referral, if you know anyone that
could use my services'. Don't make people
feel like they are on the spot. This approach
disarms people much better than asking them,
"is your company hiring" People naturally
like to do favors for people. Saying 'could you
do me a favor by referring my services to
someone'. This always places you in a better
position with them. They will feel better
about helping you. Give them 2 cards.

5. Maximize Every Per Chance Meeting

You never know when you might meet someone who can help you. Family or friends social events could produce unexpected encounters with people. Don't discount those events. So you're going to a birthday party for your friend's kid. You never know who you might meet. At a family holiday gathering, I met someone that has been instrumental in developing our business. Who would have thought this could happen by giving him a simple business card.

6. Place Yourself at the Right Place at the Right Time

Have you been to a job fair or business conference and been disappointed with the networking results? Turn the tables around. Consider volunteering to help out at the job fair or other types of events. This puts you in a better strategic position for presenting your resume or business card. Company representatives might view you differently, if they know you are willing to go the extra mile in helping them make their presence easier to manage.

Get involved by visiting the event calendars for your local city, LinkedIn, Networking Event Finders, Full Calendar, Craigslist, Speakers and Sponsors or Empowering Today's Professionals. This provides you with opportunities for giving out your business card. Volunteering for events has been a very successful resource for my business partner and me to expanding our business. Zig Ziglar, one of the most successful sales trainers in the world says "if you help enough people get what they want in life, you will get what you want in life".

7. Use Email as Your Electronic Business Card

An email sent to just 2 people, who know you, can exponentially get the word out about your business. That single email to 2 people could potentially go out to 2,000 people in less than 1 hour. It's a natural phenomenon inherent to email, called viral marketing. Your Email Signature is THE most important advertising area for you. This area is your billboard. It's also your electronic business card. This is the area where you tell people about your business.

Insert your [business] name, logo, tag line or slogan, telephone number, web site, email address and maybe your snail mail address. www.WiseStamp.com provides an awesome tool to create email signatures.

8. Use In Your Face Follow Up

After a business card exchange, ideally you want to follow up 24 to 48 hours with the new person(s) you met. Pay attention to global time zones when making follow up phone calls. This is especially crucial with sending emails. To increase the chances of your email getting noticed, read and a response, the best times to send email is Monday through Thursday 10:00AM to 2:00PM LOCAL TIME FOR YOUR CONTACT.

Although times may vary, after 2:00PM the siesta is a traditional midday sleep or time off in many countries, like Spain and many Latin American countries. Brazil stands in cultural contrast, as an exception. Afternoon sleep is also a common habit in the Philippines, China (called wujiao), Vietnam, Bangladesh (bhat-ghum meaning "rice-sleep"), India, Southern Italy, Greece, Croatia, Malta, the Middle East and North Africa. Islam suggests an afternoon sleep between Dhuhr and Asr prayers. So follow up emails may not get read during this time. Keep your note short so your email signature (tip #7) shows on the same screen.

Did you ever have a job interview or meeting with a recruiter, potential client or employer and wonder why they never called you back' 'Out of sight, out of mind' is the operative phrase to remember. Today's economic climate dictates you might be competing with 20, 50, 100 or more other people for the same position or contract. It's quite a task for people to keep track of each individual meeting.

So it's up to you to give a person a reason to call you back. Immediately after a meeting, snail mail a hand written note thanking the person for their time. Insert your business card. Now you're in the driver's seat in standing out from other people. If you get no response, do it again. Patience and persistence pays off.

9. Leverage Staff Promotions to Promote ME, Inc

Newspapers often have stories of people being promoted to high levels in different organizations. This is an opportunity for you. Consider getting some invitation size blank greeting cards. Use the Internet's search capabilities to find out the address of the company's executive offices.

Send the blank invitation type card with a hand written note sincerely congratulating a person on their promotion. Insert your business card. For the cost of a stamp, you have just made person's day and may create an impression that makes a person feel compelled to respond back to you. Make it a habit to do this once a week. Remember '6 Degrees of Separation'. You just never know . . . People open invitation type envelops faster than any others.

10. Brand Yourself With a Slogan

Print a slogan or on your business card that answers the question 'What is in it for me, if I hire you' Or What makes you different from your competition'. A catchy tag line or slogan insures people ALWAYS associate you or your company with your product or service. People remember even after the commercial is over. That's called branding.

Companies invest huge amounts of money to advertising agencies to come up with these lasting slogans. Consider doing the exact same thing on your business card. This is your insurance people remember you, after you meet. Don't just put Hortence Smiley, Accountant on your business card. Add something like "Financial Services with Integrity". A slogan makes all the difference between getting hired or not, because people will remember you long after a meeting.

Networking on Social Media

Prepare a business card signature for online Internet encounters. Similar to your email signature, add the same contact information at the end of comments made to blog or news articles. Be sincere and make sure your comment stays on topic.

This can also be done when answering questions on LinkedIn. When it comes to Facebook, comments with your business card signature on business pages is acceptable, but be very careful on personal pages. If a person is asking for help related to your expertise on their personal page, contact information may be appropriate with your comment.

Life and Networking Go Together

The trip wire for networking outcomes is separating it from everyday living. Life is an event. Any type of human interaction is an opportunity to network. We mentally stress ourselves by segregating when, where and how we are going to network.

Many years ago I replaced the word "networking" with "enjoying life". Oh sure, I refer to it by its given label when talking to people. Mentally I'm just "living in the moment". I bask in the sunlight of another person's presence. As I listen to the person, I also ask how can I help them achieve their goals. This keeps me at ease. There's no mental prepping. There's no undue pressure to get ready to be ready to network. Each person tells me what s/he wants. Then I try to meet people at their needs, by leveraging my network.

When I took my daughter to the circus or I'm having dinner at a restaurant with my wife, networking opportunities appear or they don't. It doesn't matter. I'm just "enjoying life". My all time favorite is family gatherings. My family gets on my case about it all the time. They each hate it when they see me exchanging business cards, when it's just a simple birthday party. I've been challenged with words like "what do I have to do to make you stop giving out business cards at family gatherings"? My response is "give me a referral or give me the obscene amount of money for 1 month that I pay to rent a 4 bedroom house". So far no one in my family has met either challenge. So I continue to enjoy life.

Happy trails networking . . .

Stop Networking. Start Living.

Why does networking become a chore or doesn't seem as rewarding as people promised?

Maybe it's because we're putting too much emphasis on networking. We're looking for a payback result at that pre-appointed 6:00PM event. We absolutely, positively have to make a contact at that 6:00PM to 8:30PM social mixer or that professional widget lover's association meeting.

"The World is an Event" is a previously article I published, which points out that we are surrounded by opportunities to meet people. Every day living provides an opportunity.

Years ago I worked as a plain clothes store detective, being vigilant for shop lifters. Whenever I wandered through the department store purposely looking for shop lifters, I rarely found any. When I explored the store, with a shoppers' perspective and socialized with the other employees, that is when shop lifters would appear. They would appear, because I wasn't looking. I wasn't trying so hard to find them. My job actually became easier over time.

Living everyday life and enjoying the simple passing of the day is more important, than any silly pre-appointed networking. There is only 1 simple rule to networking. Always carry business cards. That's it. So you are prepared, in case you happen to make a contact.

In the mean time take your children to the zoo, the park or the beach. Walk the dog. Water the lawn. Go out to dinner with your significant other. Stop by the travel store and plan that vacation. Perform the weekend ritual to the super shopping warehouse stores. Go bike riding. How about a horse carriage ride in Central Park or take in a movie at the local theatre. Have a social drink just for the sake of enjoying another person's company.

Living our lives everyday provides opportunities to network, but removes all the pressure. There is no pre-determined time to network. The goal is to enjoy life. There is no pressure. Focus on enjoying the here and now. Enjoy the moment. If we happen to make a connection with someone, that's the icing on the cake. Networking becomes so much more enjoyable, when we simply enjoy life. Meeting people along the way is only part of the journey.

VIDEO BONUS - How to Gain Strength from Your Network in Challenging Times

Organized by Speaker, Author and Community Leader, Rod Colon, I had the awesome opportunity of speaking at a fund raiser for the National Multiple Sclerosis Society. The theme was An Evening With Master Networkers.

If you're going through some challenging times, need a job, or new clients, in this video I share 3 lessons I learned on how to adapt, improvise and overcome.

If you wish to copy / paste a link of the video

http://www.carlereid.com/2011/05/how-to-gain-strength-from-your-network.html

About Author: Carl E. Reid

With corporate travels from the mail room to the board room, Carl E. Reid knows what it takes to be successful. He has over 40 years of business experience, including 30 years as a technology expert, 18 years as a business career coach and 20 years as a successful entrepreneur. Carl has been a professional blogger and social media strategist since 2004. In addition to being a sought after speaker and published author, he has coached and inspired hundreds of people to land jobs and start successful businesses. Carl is Executive Director for Empowering Today's Professionals, a 501(c)3 career management educational non-profit. Mr. Reid is Foreword author in fast selling book Win the Race for 21st Century by Rod Colon.

CONNECT with Carl . . .

http://www.CarlEReid.com

Twitter.com/CarlEReid

Facebook.com/SavvyIntrapreneur

Linkedin.com/in/CarlEReid

Get FREE updates via Email or RSS reader at
Library of Congress Recognized Blog
http://www.SavvyIntrapreneur.com *
Twitter.com/Intrapreneur

Tel: 201-222-5390

Email: IGetSmart@SavvyIntrapreneur.com

****
****

PLEASE WRITE A REVIEW OF THIS
BOOK

On www.Amaazon.com